AMERICAN PROTESTANTISM IN THE SPANISH ANTILLES UNTIL 1898

HISPANIC AMERICAN COLLECTION # 16

EDICIONES UNIVERSAL, Miami, Florida, 2012

GUILLERMO CABRERA LEIVA

AMERICAN PROTESTANTISM
IN THE SPANISH ANTILLES
UNTIL 1898

Copyright © 2012 by Guillermo Cabrera Leiva

―――

First Edition, 2012

EDICIONES UNIVERSAL
P.O. Box 450353 (Shenandoah Station)
Miami, FL 33245-0353. USA
Tel: (305) 642-3234   Fax: (305) 642-7978
e-mail: ediciones@ediciones.com
http://www.ediciones.com

Library of Congress Catalog Card No.: 2012937282
ISBN-10: 1-59388-234-3
ISBN-13: 978-1-59388-234-1

Cover design by Luis García Fresquet

No part of this book
may be reproduced without
written permission from the author.
For information write to Ediciones Universal

INDEX

PREFACE 7

I
CATHOLIC SPAIN AND ITS ANTILLES
IN THE XIX CENTURY 9

II
PROTESTANTISM IN LIBERAL SPAIN 21

III
AMERICAN ATTITUDE TOWARD
  THESE ISLANDS 27

IV
AMERICAN PROTESTANT MISSIONARY
MOVEMENT IN THE XIX CENTURY 41

V
AMERICAN PROTESTANTISM
IN SANTO DOMINGO 49

VI
AMERICAN PROTESTANTISM IN CUBA 59

PREFACE

This is a study on the beginnings of Protestantism in Cuba, Puerto Rico and Santo Domingo. Reading in the literature of inter-American cultural exchange revealed only scattered references to the subject which seemed to me an important chapter in the history of the Caribbean. Here, the expanding and predominantly Protestant United States came into contact and conflict with Catholic Spanish religion and culture. Therefore, it seemed logical that the Protestant church might have had some role to play in this conflict. This thesis is a result of these investigations into that subject.

The materials for this study came from widely scattered sources. For this essentially exploratory study I have not gone far beyond the resources of the University of Miami library. I am deeply indebted to the library staff for assistance in locating these materials. I am also indebted to the central administration offices of the several Protestant organizations that have responded to my inquiries and have supplied pertinent information. These are acknowledged in footnotes.

I wish here also to express my gratitude to Dr. Charlton W. Tebeau, Chairman of the History Department of the University of Miami, who directed the preparation of this thesis. Dr. Robert C. Beyer has given invaluable encouragement and assistance in that part of the work having to do with the Spanish sources.

Guillermo S. Cabrera
Coral Gables, Florida
February, 1951

I

CATHOLIC SPAIN AND ITS ANTILLES IN THE XIX CENTURY

Much of the history of Spain is a story of a struggle against non-Catholic influence at home and in her overseas empire. Protestants represented not only an alien religion, but they were also associated with the material rivals and enemies of Spain. The Catholic faith was jealously defended by Spanish rulers against all kinds of foreign inspirations, and it also became a symbol of Spanish political and territorial integrity. "Long life to the Catholic religion and down with foreigners!" became a slogan that was also a policy of the Spanish government at home and in her colonies.[1]

Protestant nations such as England and Holland disputed and finally destroyed Spanish maritime supremacy and its

---

[1] Roque E. Garrigó, *America para los Americanos*, New York, The Garrick Press, 1910, p. 132.

commercial monopoly in the Caribbean. Famous pirates such as Jacques de Sores, "a devout Huguenot"[2] became Protestant heroes where depredations on Spanish property were justified on both national and religious grounds. To the Spanish authorities and their colonists such men were no less than unholy robbers and bandits. Consequently, the few Protestants that entered the Spanish dominions during the years of Spanish power and the rigorous years of the Inquisition were mostly captured corsairs and foreign merchants.[3]

Small wonder then that Protestants and Protestant religious agencies made no significant impression upon the lives of the people in the Spanish speaking Antilles before the nineteenth century, and that very slowly and under the handicap of considerable official opposition which was both political and religious.

Puerto Rico, for example, knew the rigor of the Inquisition before any other island in the Caribbean. Bishop Alonso Manso organized the Catholic tribunal in San Juan in 1519, with no limits to his personal discretion.[4] It is presumed that the smallness of Puerto Rico reduced to the minimum the Protestant interference from outside, and made

---

[2] Hugh Bradley, *Havana, Cinderella City*, Garden City, New York, D. Doran and Co. 1941, p. 67.

[3] Clarence H. Haring, The Spanish Empire in America, New York, Oxford University Press, 1947. p. 203.

[4] Robert McLean and Grace Petrie Williams. *Old Spain in New America*, New York, Association Press, 1916, p. 112.

it easier for Spain to keep strict control of foreigners. The English Protestant missionary, Thomas Coke, almost three centuries later, in 1811, complained of the exclusiveness of the Catholic church in that island. He considered that such absolute control had only the consequence of perpetuating superstition and ignorance.[5] Even sugar technicians, if Protestants, were not permitted to enter that Antille until about 1828.[6]

The liberal ideas of some of the native leaders of the independence movement of 1868 gave some promises of religious tolerance. The most conspicuous thinker of that political movement, Eugenio María de Hostos, was a frank defender of Protestant principles.[7] Another leader of that revolution, Dr. Emeterio Betances, a physician, had also shared the tolerant ideas of Hostos. In 1865 Betances had written the "Ten Commandments of the Free Man", a set of civil rights for the people of Puerto Rico where freedom of religion, among other liberties, was included.[8]

Unfortunately for any promise of toleration for Protestants, that armed movement was soon crushed by Spain, and the era of colonial status and absolute Spanish

---

[5] Thomas Coke, *A History of the West Indies*, Londin, T. Blandshard, 1811, 3. Volumes, Vol. III, p. 102.

[6] Vincenzo Petrullo, *Puerto Rican Paradox*, Philadelphia, University of Pennsylvania Press, 1947, p. 42.

[7] Eugenio M. de Hostos, *Moral Social*, Madrid, Imprenta de Bailly-Baillere e Hijos, 1906, p. 168.

[8] Vincenzo Petrullo, *op. cit.*, p. 45.

control was extended to the end of the nineteenth century in Puerto Rico.[9] This policy of total and severe exclusion of non-Catholic elements explains the complete absence of American missionary activity in the island, prior to 1898.[10]

The Spanish regime in the Dominican territory ended in 1821. Up to that year the same system of Spanish political and Catholic religious monopoly operated there. Beginning with 1822, after some months of ephemeral independence, the Spanish speaking part of the island was invaded and subjugated by Jean Pierre Boyer, Negro dictator of Haiti. His regime was to last until 1844, the year of the definitive political liberation of Santo Domingo, and the creation of a new nation known as the Dominican Republic. The Dominicans did not succeed in establishing a stable government. Fears of new Haitian invasions, and the refusal of American statesmen to recognize the young state, made them ask repeatedly for reannexation to Spain from 1844 to 1862. At this latter date Spanish Queen Isabella II signed the

---

[9] Arthur D. Hall, *Cuba and Our New Possessions*, New York, Street and Smith, Publishers, 1898, p. 25.

[10] This is corroborated by *"The Encyclopedia of Missions"*, by Rev. Henry Otis Dwight, et. Al., New York, Funk and Wagnalls Co., 1904, *World Statistics of Christian Missions*, by Harlan F. Beach and Burton St. John, Committee of Reference and Counsel of the Foreign Missions Conference of North America, New York, 1916, and Interpretative Statistical Survey of the World Mission of the Christian Church.

royal decree of annexation, and the Dominican General Santana proclaimed the new status on March 18, 1861.[11]

The new colonial experience was not different from the first. From 1861 to 1865 the regime of Spain in Santo Domingo was characterized by a renewal of the policy of absolutism and intolerance toward foreigners and alien religions.[12] The American Protestants who had migrated to the town of Samaná under the Boyer regime suffered offenses and persecutions during that period, and their religious services were forbidden.[13]

When a new uprising expelled the Spanish troops in 1865, and installed a native regime in Santo Domingo, the influence of Spanish political power was finally gone, but there remained here, as in other places of Latin America, an essentially Spanish culture, reflected principally in the intellectual, social and religious life of the native people. But increasingly North American political and economic influences penetrated the island and with them increasing Protestant ideas and interests.

---

[11] Parker, New York, International Missionary Council, 1938. This is also confirmed by Dr. Angel Archilla in his article on the origin of the Protestant work in that island, in Puerto Rico Evangélico, V. 38, No. 1052, p. 4, and also in a personal letter from this writer to the author of this thesis.

Gordon Ireland, *Boundaries, Possessions nd Conflicts in Central and North America and the Caribbean*, Cambridge, Mass., Harvard University Press, 1941, p. 48.

[12] Mary Treudley, *The United States and Santo Domingo, 1789-1866*, Worcester, Mass., 1916, p. 257.

[13] Emilio Rodriguez, *"Samaná, Pasado y Porvenir"*, Editorial Montalvo, Ciudad Trujillo, 1945, p. 33.

In Cuba the story is not much different. Her geographic situation, her natural richness, and the political and economical advantages for the Spanish crown made that Antille the favorite possession of the mother country, much more so after Spain's loss of her other colonies on the American continent. Repression and intolerance were the rule in Cuba throughout the 19th century, although this attitude was modified in regard to religion during the last two decades of that century.[14] There is no evidence of any Protestant activity before the year 1870, and after that time there are testimonies of official opposition to Protestantism, even to the very end of the Spanish dominion in the island.[15]

In the first quarter of the 19th century every visitor's baggage was carefully searched for heretical books, which, if found, were invariably confiscated and destroyed.[16] At that time two liberal Catholic thinkers, Father Felix Varela and lawyer José Antonio Saco were also expelled from the island. This was an era of drastic measures against everything implying liberalism. Spain was using her rich colony as a vast source of goods and money; here ideas were dangerous weapons against the peaceful maintenance of that colonial status.

---

[14] Episcopalians and Baptists were already active in Cuba since 1883 and 1885.

[15] The victims of Maine explosion were not permitted to be buried with Protestant ceremonies in 1898.

[16] James Hyde Clark, *Cuba and the Fight for Freedom*. Philadelphia, Globe Bible Publishing Co., 1896, p. 186.

Early in 1828 a Protestant preacher of Boston, Reverend Abiel Abbot, visited the western portion of Cuba. His account of his travels in Cuba reflects a complete absence of Protestantism in the island.[17] The same testimony comes from Joseph John Gurney who visited Havana in 1840. Gurney wrote to Henry Clay that "no Protestant worship is tolerated in the island, not even in the house of the British consul".[18] In 1859 Richard Henry Dana in his book "To Cuba and Back" gives similar evidence of intolerance.[19]

The American consul at Havana informed Rachel W. Moore, a Quaker preacher from Philadelphia visiting the island in 1863, that even five persons holding a Protestant prayer-meeting in a private room could be sent to jail by Spanish authorities, on the ground of offense against the Catholic hierarchy.[20]

The official intolerance was also extended to other organizations not precisely Protestants. In 1870 several lodges of Florida, Illinois and New York protested before

---

[17] Abiel Abbot, *Letters written in the interior of Cuba*, Boston, Bowles and Dearborn. 1829.

[18] Joseph John Gurney. *Familiar Letters to Henry Clay of Kentucky, Describing A Winter in the West Indies*, New York, Press of M. Day & Co., 1840, p. 162.

[19] Richard Henry Dana, *To Cuba and Back,* Boston, Ticknor and Friends,1859, p.74.

[20] George Truman, *Journal of Rachel Wilson Moore*, Philadelphia, Publisher, T. Ellwood Zell, 1867, p. 33.

American authorities the persecution and murder of some Cuban masons.[21]

(Wherever the Spanish regime existed, the Catholic clergy had all powers to act against freedom of thought.) "Religion and Church influence developed to a point that made it easily the most powerful social force in Latin American history", said G. Desdevices du Dezert in an article on the Spanish church in America.[22] The main factors enumerated by this author as supporting that power are the Church organization, its influence over the State, and the Inquisition. This last factor was not in operation in the Antilles during most of the nineteenth century, but it was its influence over the state which was most important then. According to Bailey Diffie, the official policy of the Church was to "limit education to those chosen by it, liberty to those who conformed, ideas to those it approved".[23]

That situation, nevertheless, was not the same in regard to morals of the clergy. Far from a severe regime of life, the Cuban Catholic priesthood was generally considered impious and pharisaical. In 1838 the celebrated writer Domingo del Monte, in an interview with the English representative investigating the social conditions of Negroes in Cuba at that time, maintained that the corruption of the

---

[21] José Ignacio Rodríguez, *Origen y Desenvolvimiento de la idea de la Anexión de la Isla de Cuba a los Estados Unidos de América*, Habana, La Propaganda Literaria, 1900, p. 517.

[22] *Revue Hispanique*, V. 39, p. 112.

[23] Bailey W. Diffie, *Latin American Civilization*, Harrisburgh, Pa., Stackpole, 1945, p. 577.

Catholic clergy gave support to the advisibility of introducing the Protestant church in the island.[24]

Education was in the hands of the Roman church too. It was scholastic and impractical. According to Russell H. Fitzgibbon, no public schools existed in the island before 1842, and those existing after that time were "nothing even approaching the free school system of the United States".[25]

Some of the best pictures of the Cuban clergy during the past century were obtained by several American and European travelers, allowing always for their national and religious views. James Anthony Proude, an Englishman touring the West Indies almost at the end of the Spanish domination in Cuba, gave a valuable testimony of the laziness of priests in Cuba. "I inquired about famous preachers", he says, "I was told that there was no preaching in Havana, famous or otherwise".[26] A parallel observation is left by Rev. Abbott many years earlier, after watching Catholic ceremonies whose process a sincere Protestant Christian could not approve.

In 1851 the Danish Protestant, Fredericka Bremer, after some months traveling in the United States, wished to visit

---

[24] José Antonio Saco, *Historia de la Esclavitud Africana*, Habana, Cultural S,A., 1938, V. IV, p.328.

[25] Russell H. Fitzgibbon, *Cuba and the United States*, Menasha, Wis., The Collegiate Press, 1936, p. 45.

[26] James A. Froude, *The English in the West Indies*, New York, C. Scribner's Sons, 1900, p. 304.

Cuba, which she did in February of that year. In a brief and plain statement Miss Bremer pointed out the condition of Cuban clergy as "being quite unclerical, the greater number living in open defiance of their vows".[27]

The explanation has been offered by a contemporary American writer that many discredited Spanish clergy come to the colonies with royal orders to be installed in ecclesiastical positions.[28] The lack of religious devotion in the Catholic population may be attributed to this, as observed by Demoticus Philatetes in 1856.[29] William L. Jay, as he described it during his trip to Cuba in 1871, thought it was possible "to count on the fingers of one hand" the male persons he saw attending services, or engaged in any Church activity".[30]

Even their limited knowledge of the vital influence of the Protestant and Catholic clergy in other part of the western hemisphere, notably in the United States, seems not to have stirred them out of their lethargy and lack of religious zeal and concern for their people's social and religious welfare. Probably loyalty to Spain was the most remarkable characteristic of the clergy in Cuba. As Willis

---

[27] Fredericka Bremer, *The Homes of the New World*, Haspers and Brother, 1954, V. II, p. 374.

[28] Wade Crawford Barclay, *Greater Good Neighbor Policy*, Chicago, Willet, Clark & Company, 1945, p. 229.

[29] Demoticus Philatetes, *Yankee Travels Through the Island of Cuba*, New York, D. Appleton and Co., 1871, p. 167.

[30] William L. Jay, *My Winter in Cuba*, E. P. Dutton & Co., 1871, p. 167.

Johnson has described it, the priesthood of the island was absolutely against the revolution and in favor of maintaining the sovereignty of the Spanish crown in Cuba.[31] Almost at the time of the American intervention in the island, when the last phase of the revolution swept the interior of Cuba, Pope Leo XIII expressed his disapprobation of the insurrection.[32] According to a Cuban writer, "the head of the Catholic congregation considered the Spanish *children*, and the Cubans *stepchildren*.[33]

This association of the official Catholic hierarchy in Cuba with opposition to Cuban independence, and the feeling that Cubans were being relegated to subordinate status in Spanish thinking tended further to weaken the position of the Catholic Church and possible to open the way to non-Catholic religious organizations to penetrate the island.

---

[31] *The History of Cuba,* (4 Vols.) New York, B. F. Buck & Co.. Inc,. 1920, IV, p. 26.

[32] Evangelina Cisneros, *The Story of Evangelina Cisneros*, New York, Continental Publishing Company, 1898, p. 48.

[33] Fitzgibbon, *op. cit.*, p. 23.

II

PROTESTANTISM IN LIBERAL SPAIN

Not until the middle of the 19th Century did liberalism in any form appear in Spain which may be said to have eased the way for the introduction of non-Catholic and non Spanish ideas into Spain and her colonies. In 1868 a revolution headed by General Juan Prim, and supported by a large group of liberal lawyers and writers, seized power after a successful blow against the government of Isabella II. That momentous strike brought Spain a good deal more than merely a new political structure. A sense of democracy was awakened, and with it a desire for a less autocratic and intolerant government.

Perhaps the noblest figure in all that political revolt was Don Emilio Castelar, an orator and writer of high moral qualifications. His personal interest in religious freedom was evident throughout his ardous labors during drafting of the constitution. "In the name of the Evangel", Castelar said, in the session of April 12, 1869, "I come here to ask that you write in your fundamental code religious freedom, which is liberty, fraternity, equality among men."[34]

The revolutionaries, even when favoring a new monarch after Prim's proclamation, earnestly supported the new constitution. The document voted in 1869, if not a perfect realization of the liberal principles of its sponsors, was indeed a great legal novelty in Spain. Its second article declared, "No person shall be molested in the territory of Spain for his religious opinions, nor for the exercise of his particular worship, saving the respect due to Christian morality".[35] Nevertheless, a following clause destroyed any hope of complete religious toleration by specifying that no other ceremonies nor manifestations in public will be permitted other than those of the religion of the State (Roman Catholicism)".[36]

In 1874 the Bourbons were restored to the throne of Spain, the Constitution of 1869 nullified, and the brief era of liberalism came to an end. The repercussion in America of the liberal interlude was not great. Notwithstanding, something was obtained by Anglo-American Protestants in Cuba and Puerto Rico, Spanish territories where the provisions of the Constitution also were extended. English-

---

[34] Frank E. Manuel, *The Politics of Modern Spain*, New York, McGraw-Hill Book Co. Inc., 1938. p. .9.

[35] Frederick Meyrick, *The Church in Spain*, New York.J. Pott & Co., 1892, p. 444.

[36] *Ibid.*

speaking residents of Ponce, Puerto Rico, took advantage of the new situation, and organized a small Episcopal church under the care of the Bishop of Antigua, Virgin Islands, in 1869.[37] That congregation, and a small school for the children of Anglo-American residents in Vieques,[38] were the only agencies of Protestantism in the island of Borinquen during the Spanish domination. It is also remarkable that this was the first Protestant mission ever permitted by the Government of Madrid in any of his dominions.

The mission of Ponce was supported by British contributions and the English Queen Victoria gave the frame of the chapel and the bell,[39] the site being donated by a Schuck family of Ponce.[40] Its services were tolerated until 1874. After that date it was necessary through the good offices of the British Government to secure special permission for the church to remain open, provided only that it would never ring the bell, nor its preacher deliver services in Spanish language, nor any native of Puerto Rico be admitted in the congregation.[41]

---

[37] Arthur R. Gray, *The New World*, New York, The Domestic and Foreign Missionary Society, 1920, p. 99.

[38] Paul G. Miller, *Historia de Puerto Rico*, Nueva York, Rand McNally y Cia., 1922, p. 466.

[39] W. A. Roberts, *Lands of the Inner Sea*, NewYork, Coward McCann, 1948. p. 107.

[40] Puerto Rican Reconstruction Administration, *Puerto Rico, a Guide to the Island of Borinquen*, New York, The University Society Inc., 1940, p.243.

[41] Archilla, letter to the author of this thesis.

As a coincidence, the year 1868 witnessed revolutionary movement in Spain, Puerto Rico and Cuba. In those revolts the political principles involved were more or less, the same. Yet the situation of Cuba had particular characteristics. Unlike the short uprising in the Puerto Rican mountains of Lares, Cuban rebels were able to fight a long war of ten years. One consequence was a decade of hate and persecution of Cubans and a strict vigilance of Anglo-American visitors.

The continuous coming of armed expeditions from the United States, often including United States citizens and equipped with American arms, created an atmosphere not exactly propitious for the flourishing of foreign ideas, religious or otherwise.

(Protestant activities were practically non-existent in Spain before the Revolution of 1868 when the reform "dared to lift its head in the Peninsula" after many centuries of silence.[42] Attempts to enter Spain has been made by Protestant English people since 1816, but no success was possible against the firm opposition of the official church. During the years of the first Spanish Republic (February, 1873 to December, 1874) some progress was visible, and Spanish figures like Don Cipriano Tornos of Madrid were soon considered the most able leaders of the native

---

[42] Francis E. Clark and Harriet A. Clark, *The Gospel in Latin Lands*, New York, The Macmillan Company, 1909, p.141.

Protestants there.[43] From the reports of those Spanish missions it appears that neither American nor English missionaries were able to make any important progress there, and their efforts were relaxed.)

Neither Cubans nor Puerto Ricans received any sort of propaganda or literature from the Spanish Protestantism in the years of the Spanish Republic. The evangelical movement in the mother country was too weak to undertake any type of work outside the limited areas of its local stations. It remained for English-speaking people and natives of the island living in the United States who were converts to Protestantism, to penetrate for the first time the Spanish possessions in the Caribbean.

---

[43] *Ibid.*, p. 145.

III

AMERICAN ATTITUDE TOWARD THESE ISLANDS

The islands of the Caribbean have always been of great interest to the United States. Strategically, their interest is beyond any doubt. Economically, the Greater Antilles are still of primary importance to the American nation. During the nineteenth century there were instances when the destiny of these islands seemed to be in the hands of the United States.

The acquisition of Cuba, either through purchase or military force, was a topic of wide political discussion in Washington throughout the last century. Early in 1818 the Spanish authorities in Cuba saw fit to provide the measures against adventurers "armed and protected in the United

States".[44] The cession of Florida to the United States in 1819 also gave basis for fear of an American attack upon the island.[45]

In 1823 President Jefferson had shown his favorable attitude on the adding of Cuba to the national area of the Union.[46] The same year John Quincy Adams used the word "annexation" for the first time, in a letter dealing with the possibility of the acquisition of Cuba.[47] Some proposals in regard to this matter were discussed in the Congress of the United States during the thirties.[48]

By this time the American influence in Cuba largely supplanted that of England, because of the similar interests of the slaveholders in this island and in the southern states of North America.[49]

As time passed the United States became the base for more intense activity against the Spanish policy in Cuba. Some groups of Cuban exiles in the United States were already publishing revolutionary literature in New York and

---

[44] Luis Marino Pérez, *Guide to the materials for the American history in Cuban archives*, Washington, D.C., Carnegie Institute of Washington, 1907, p. 66.

[45] *Ibid.*

[46] José Ignacio Rodríguez, *Origen y Desenvolvimiento de la Idea de la Anexión de la Isla de Cuba a los Estados Unidos de América*, Habana, La Propaganda Literaria. 1900, p. 52.

[47] *Ibid.*, p. 56.

[48] Pérez, *op. cit.*, p. 38.

[49] James Norton Callahan, *Cuba and International Relations, a historical study in American diplomacy*, Baltimore, The Johns Hopkins Press, 1899, p. 14.

Philadelphia.⁵⁰ The entire decade of the forties was agitated by conspiracies in the island, and fears of invasions from Northern ports. The consequence was, among others, an increasing suspicion of American consuls in Cuba, and much effort to shut out the influence of American republican ideas among the islanders. In 1844 the Spanish Ambassador in Washington suggested to the Foreign Minister in Madrid that he cease giving permission to Cubans to study in the United States.

The year 1850 was extremely agitated by the Lopez expedition, which had as its aim the overthrow of Spanish rule by initiating a revolution in the island, and was supposedly inspired and helped by American authorities. A new decade of anti-Spanish propaganda then started in the United States. In retaliation and defense, American vessels were zealously checked all around the island, and more than one incident provoked an American protest before the Spanish governor in Cuba.

The revolutionary movement initiated in the island in October, 1868, was inspired by liberal ideas, some taken from France, and some from the United States. Its agents in North America soon began to work for the recognition of belligerent status for the rebels. Some Americans such as Representative Thomas Fitch from Nebraska, early in 1870

---

[50] José A. Saco edited in New York a weekly publication named "La Verdad", associated with his countryman Father Felix Varela, and they also published "El Mensajero Semanal" in Philadelphia during the thirties. These periodicals were destined to spread liberal ideas among Cubans, and to inform others about the political situation of Cuba.

proposed such legal action in Congress at Washington.[51] The education of the leaders of that movement, and the political structure of the insurrectionary government assured religious liberty, and identified the rebellion, in many aspects, with the American Revolution of 1776.[52]

Circumstances were not favorable for American recognition at that time. The seventies were an era of "unrestrained terror"in the island, a time when American citizens in Cuba were seen as "spies and intruders" by Spanish authorities.[53]

If the idea of recognition of Cuban independence had occasional support in the mind of some American statesmen, the possibility of annexation was almost uninterruptedly cherised by eminent figures from Jefferson to McKinley. Some islanders of prestige favored the annexation on the ground of the Spanish inability to govern the colony.[54] According to William Cullent Bryant, who visited Cuba in

---

[51] Pérez, *op.cit.*, p. 130.

[52] Top leaders of the revolution, like Carlos M. de Céspedes, Ignacio Agramonte, and Salvador Cisneros, were Masons and free-thinkers, as were Washington, Jefferson and Thomas Paine.

[53] Herminio Portell-Vilá, *Historia de Cuba en sus relaciones con España y los Estados Unidos*, Jesús Montero, Editor, Habana, 1939, V. 2, p. 350.

[54] José Antonio Fernández de Castro, *Medio siglo de Historia Colonial de Cuba*, Ricardo Veloso, Editor. Habana, 1923. This work contains humdreds of letters of eminent Cubans like Miguel Aldama, Gaspar Betancourt, Domingo del Monte, Rafael Montoro, Felix Varela, etc., expressing this viewpoint on the subject.

1850, "Creoles would be glad to see the Island annexed to the United States."[55]

The most famous and serious opponent of annexation among Cubans was José Antonio Saco, a lawyer and writer of liberal principles. His arguments were published during the fifties, and carried weight enough to counteract somewhat the efforts of the annexationists. He based his anti-annexationism largely on the defense of Cuba's Hispanic characteristics, which might be lost amid a fast-growing Anglo-Saxon population.[56]

An extensive checking of the arguments for and against annexation does not reveal religion as a factor of such importance, though occasionally such argument do appear. Travelers like Richard B, Kimball, a Protestant author and businessman who visited Cuba in 1850, wrote that the most important reason for annexation as told by "serious and reflecting Cubans", was derived from the moral and religious corruption in the island. Kimball approved annexation as the door for a free Bible, a free pulpit, and a free press.[57] Another opinion of the same nature was given

---

[55] Callahan, *op. cit.*, p.223.

[56] This argument is widely expounded in *Contra la anexión*, by José A. Saco, Habana, Cultural S.A., 1931.

[57] Richard M. Kimball, *Cuba and the Cubans,* New York, Samuel Hueston, 1850, p. 158. Mr. Kimball was a devoted Presbyterian and a profound student of the Bibhle. He was a lawyer, and a prolific writer. Unlike Saco, Kimball was educated in a Puritan and Anglo-American environment, and was a dynamic and enterprising colonizer. He founded the town of Kimball, Texas, and was one of the stockholders of the "American West India Company",
(continued...)

by Maturin M. Ballou, a visitor to Cuba in 1854. Being a "firm Protestant", though not a fanatic, Ballou observed some differences between religious conditions in Cuba and those prevailing in North America, and concluded by favoriting and predicting annexation. "Modern churches", he said, "dedicated to pure Christianity, would rise (if Annexation comes) their lofty spires and point towards heaven beside those ancient and time-eaten Cathedrals."[58]

American commercial interests in Cuba were growing with the years. In 1837, when the first railway was inaugurated in the province of Havana, the engineeer and the jobbers of that enterprise were American citizens. From America came the steam engines for sugar factories, so largely developed in the island.[59] Steam and the telegraph were changing the rhythm of business and commerce in the fifties.[60] Dozens of American land-owners had been living in the provinces of Havana and Matanzas since the twenties,[61] although it was not until the close of the first war for independence in 1878 that great investments of

---

[57] (...continued)
an organization created by William Cazneau in New York in 1862 with the aim to promote American investments in Santo Domingo. His attitude toward Cuba may be considered typical of "good-faith", American expansionists at that time.

[58] Maturin M. Ballou, *History of Cuba*, Boston, Phillips, Sdampson and Co., 1854, p.200.

[59] Leland H.Jenks, *Our Cuban Colony*, New York, Vanguard Press, 1928, p. 19.

[60] Ballou, *op. cit.*, p. 198.

[61] Abiel Abbot, *Letters written in the interior of Cuba*, Boston, Bowles and Dearbon, 1829. This author visiting Cuba in 1828 repeatedly mentions names of American proprietors whose farms he was invited to see during his stay in that Spanish colony.

American capital were poured into this Antille, largely in the sugar industry.[62]

Most of the Americans residing in Cuba were Protestants, but there is no trace of their having used their citizenship or their religious affiliations to secure any special privilege from the Spanish authorities in Cuba. The government of the United States does not appear to have taken advantage of these minorities in Cuba to seek special privileges of worship from the colonial authorities there. It seems that any appeal those Americans in Cuba made was on behalf of their economic interests, many times in peril of destruction by continous conflicts and revolts.

Americans were not less interested in Santo Domingo. It was also for the United States a desirable spot in the Caribbean. Unlike Cuba and Puerto Rico, Santo Domingo became free from Spain in 1821, and from that time, particularly after the Haitian occupation of the entire island in 1822-1843, the United States had all kinds of opportunities to become master of that small country. Nevertheless, some factors made the Government of Washington practice a policy of abstention in Dominican affairs up to 1870, and, in spite of the troubled political development of that republic, Americans did not take advantage of that favorable circumstance until after the American Civil War.

---

[62] Janks, *op. Cit.* P. 35.

In 1844, the year of the Dominican independence from Haiti, the Government of the young Spanish-speaking country sent Jose M. Caminero to Washington to obtain American recognition. For that purpose President Tyler ordered an investigation of conditions in Santo Domingo, in 1845, and John Hogan was sent on that mission. During the following nine years four more American envoys were dispatched to Santo Domingo in order to inform Washington about the general conditions of the country.[63]

The failure to recognize Santo Domingo's independence was due largely to racial prejudices then shared by leading American statesmen. As in the case of Cuba, religious motives did not have any decisive importance in political circles of the United States at that time. "These two little States (Haiti and Santo Domingo)", according to an American author, "were treated practically as footballs by the parties, pro and con, the domestic issue of Slavery in the United States".[64]

Travelers like J. Dennis Harris, who arrived in Santo Domingo in 1860, presented an attractive picture of the Dominican territory, as the ideal place to settle American

---

[63] Mary Treudley. *The United States and Santo Domingo*. Worcester, Mass., 1916. p. 234, 235. 244. William R. Manning, *Diplomatic Correspondence of the United States, Inter-American Affairs,* Division of Latin American Affairs, Washington, D.C., 1935, V. 6.

[64] Melvin M. Knight, *The Americans in Santo Domimgo*, New York, Vanguard Press, 1928, p. 2.

colonists "under official American protection."[65] This author, an educated Negro, was an enthusiastic promotor of the idea of colonizing the Spanish part of that island with American Negro families. The idea, supported in the American Congress by Senator Francis F. Blair in that year and favored by some other political figures like Senators Doolittle, of Wisconsin, and Bingham, of Michigan, was never popular.[66]

The Spanish re-occupation of Santo Domingo occurred in the years of the American Civil War, and apart from a formal protest to the Government at Madrid, no direct action was taken on that occasion on behalf of the principles of the Monroe Doctrine. Nevertheless, a few years after the end of the Spanish occupation the recognition of the small Caribbean republic was granted by President Grant. Paradoxically, it was during Grant's administration that definite plans for annexation were completed. In November 29, 1869, with the entire compliance of the Dominican Government, the question of incorporating the country in the United States was submitted to the islanders through a referendum. In spite of being favorable to the annexation, the electoral survey was finally rejected by the American

---

[65] J. Dennis Harris, *A summer on the borders of the Caribbean sea*, New York, A. B. Burdick, Publisher, 1860, p. x.

[66] *Ibid.*, p. ix.

Congress after a careful investigation, on charges of falsehhod and violence.[67]

Both American official agents and private travelers reported the existence of religious tolerance in the republic since the year following its inauguration. Although diplomatic correspondence was largely on political and economic matters, religion was sometimes mentioned. In 1850 the American agent Benjamin Green suggested to Secretary of State Clayton the convenience of a treaty in which religious tolerance for American citizens would be secured, since in spite of a positive state of tolerance, the Catholic church was the official one of the country, the formal assurance being necessary to "place religious freedom beyond the caprice of the government as William Cazneay's report indicated in 1854.[68]

The question of annexation was kept alive throughout the century. De Benneville Keim, visiting Santo Domingo in the seventies, believed that the destiny of all the island of the Caribbean was American. "The influence of American institutions, he said, "daily becomes more deeply felt, and as time moves on we observe its mysterious operations more openly exhibited." [69]

---

[67] Max Henriquez Ureña, *Los Yanquis en Santo Domingo*, Madrid, M. Aguilar, Editor, 1930, p. 19.

[68] Manning, *op. cit.*, pp. 67, 124.

[69] De Benneville Randolph Keim, *Sketches of San Domingo*, Philadelphia, Claxton, Remsen & Haffelfinger, 1870,p.m 128.

Perhaps one of the most colorful reports on the Catholic point of view on annexation was given by Samuel Hazard, author and artist traveling in Santo Domingo in 1873. During a conversation with the Vicar General of the Roman Catholic Church in that republic, the prelate disliked annexation on the ground that his church would no longer be the official cult of the State. After Hazard's reply giving assurance of the absolute tolerance for Catholics under American rule, the Bishop cynically complained of his duty to tolerate others, too.[70]

Nevertheless, it is the same Hazard who stated that no religious intolerance could be discovered in Santo Domingo in that year, and that the American Baptist and Methodist Negroes who had come there in 1824 were living in peace and harmony among the Catholics.[71]

A good many American travelers were attracted by the advertising originated by some steamship companies of New York, operating between this port and Santo Domingo. Firms like "Santo Domingo Line" initiated a regular service in 1870 between New York and Samaná and Puerto Plata, in Dominican territory, at a price of one hundred and sixty dollars "gold". The tourist propaganda appealed to those interested in "a mild climate during the winter and spring

---

[70] Samuel Hazard, *Santo Domingo, Past and Present*, New York, Harper & Brothers, 1873, p. 227.

[71] *Ibid.*, p. 486.

months", and companies like the Ward Line published in the same year a booklet on "Life in the West Indies".[72]

The name of Puerto Rico was generally mentioned together with the other Antilles, but it was not so much the special object of diplomatic arrangements nor the subject of much political discussion in Washington before the nineties. There were, nevertheless, some instances during the past century where American authorities participated directly in Puerto Rican affairs.

The attack against some pirates in the harbor of San Juan, in 1816, by the American commodore, David Porter, was perhaps the first occurrence of importance in which the name of the United States was prominently linked to Puerto Rico. Six years later a more famous military enterprise involved a well known American political figure in Puerto Rico events. This was the armed expedition led by Aaron Burr and the European General Louis Ducodray Holstein. The expedition, totally crushed a short time after its departure from Philadelphia, was designed to expel the Spaniards from the island with the cooperation of the natives, and to establish a republican government in Puerto Rico.[73]

---

[72] New York City WPA Writer's Project, *A Maritime History of New York*, New Yorh, 1941, p.199.

[73] Gorden Ireland, *Boundaries, Possessions and Conflicts in Central and North America and the Caribbean*, Cambridge, Mass., Harvard University Press, 1941, p. 353.

During the uprising at Lares, in 1868, the independents leader Betances had the collaboration of the American citizens: Dr. J. J. Hanna, and Matthew Bruckman, both captured by the Spaniards. Mr. Hanna was permitted to return to New York, but Bruckman had to face a sentence of death.[74]

From scattered evidences it is known that some American families were living in Puerto Rico during the nineteenth century. Place like Ponce, San Juan, Vieques Islands, and Arroyo, had American residents before the mid century. It was in Arroyo that Samuel F. B. Morse, the famous inventor of the telegraph, spent a short vacation in 1859, and established a telegraphic line in that year.[75]

---

[74] Arthur D. Hall, *Cuba and Our New Possessiions*, NewYork, Street and Smith, Publishers, 1898, p. 25.

[75] Paul G. Miller, *Historia de Puertro Rico*, Nueva York, Rand McNally y Cia., 1922, p. 351.

IV

AMERICAN PROTESTANT MISSIONARY MOVEMENT IN THE XIX CENTURY

The New England Puritan Cotton Mather, as early as 1699, expressed his desire to spread Protestant doctrines throughout the Spanish Indies. His plan took form when he ordered the printing of a short book in Spanish, containing cardinal principles of the Christian faith, and "irresistible sentences of the Scriptures" in order "to bomb those kingdoms with the word of God".[76]

Mather's friend, Samuel Sewall, also from Massachusetts, was interested in the same enterprise. He ordered a Spanish Bible from London, and a copy of the famous "Destrucción de las Indias" by Father Las Casas. Like his colleague Mather, Sewall tried by several methods to

---

[76] Harry Bernstein, *Origins of Inter-American Interest*, Philadelphia, Univ, of Pennsylvania Press, 1945, p. 69.

introduced Protestant ideas in the islands of the Caribbean. He had the opportrunity to talk to Don Carlos Sucre, an ancestor of Bolívar who visited Boston in 1709, and discussed with him the possibilities of preaching the Gospel of Christ in the other America.[77]

Some other religious leaders of New England, like Roger Williams and John Higginston, "were early convinced of the religious necessity of driving the Spaniards from America".[78]

It is needless to repeat that those plans were never accomplished, since the Kings of Spain prohibited much contact between Spanish-Americans and non-Catholic countries. Even commercial relations were radically avoided before 1801, and it was not until 1818 that free commerce with foreigners was definitely legalized by the Crown.[79] In its monopolistic legislation, the Government at Madrid tried not only to preserve its commercial privileges in the Caribbean, but to prevent outside influences from "heretic" nations.

The organized and united missionary movement in the United States did not appear vigorously until after the American Civil War, when the necessity to "Christianize"

---

[77] *Ibid.*, p. 70.

[78] E. Taylor Parks, *Colombia and the United States, 1765-1934*, Durham, N.C., Duke Universiy Press, 1935, p. 35.

[79] Gordon Ireland, *Boundaries, Possessions and Conflicts in Central and North America and the Caribbean*, Cambridge, Mass., Harvard University Press, 1941, p. 325.

the ex-slave states was generally felt by the northern churches, and also gave impulse to foreign missionary work. Yet we find scattered American missionaries like Reverend Joseph John Gurney, from the Friend's Society, trying to penetrate the exclusive fields of the Spanish Catholicism in the Caribbean during the last century. Spending a week in Havana in 1840, Gurney reported that his journey was in the exclusive character of a minister of the Gospel, his primary object being to preach "the glad tidings of peace and salvation to my fellow men, and to persons of every class, conditions, and party in the West Indies".[80]

The abolitionist and traveler J. Dennis Harris, deeply interested in developing American Negro colonization in the tropics, suggested in 1860 to the Reverend George Duffield, of the Presbyterian Church in Detroit, that he initiate a missionary movement in the Spanish islands of the Caribbean, specially in Santo Domingo. The idea was warmly received by Rev. Duffield, who wished his church to consider it during its coming annual assembly.[81]

But nothing definite was done in the Spanish-speaking Antilles at that time. The coming of the Civil War in the

---

[80] Joseph John Gurney, *Familiar Letters to Henry Clay of Kentucky, Describing a Winter In the West Indies*, New York, Press of M. Day & Co., 1840, p. 3.

[81] *The National Encyclopedia of American Biography*, New York, James T. White & Co., 1909, V. III, p. 505. J. Dennis Harris, *A summer on the borders of the Caribbean sea,* New York, A. B. Burdick, Publisher, 1860, p. 179. Henry Otis Dwight *et al.*, The Encyclopedia of Missions Descriptive, Historical, Biographical, *Statistical,* New York, Funk & Wagnalls Co., 1904.

United States, with all its material problems and calamities, made the home boards of American churches much too busy to plan a well directed foreign movement before the eighties. Nevertheless, it is during and after the American Civil War that many of the great international religious enterprises had their origins. Methodists, for instance, organized their women's missionary society and their board of church extension early in the seventies.[82]

Presbyterians reunited their forces in a general assembly in Philadelphia in 1870, to support the work of their Board of Foreign missions.[83] Bodies like the Missionary Society of the Protestant Episcopal Church had been created in 1860, although most of them did not enlarge their sphere of activity until 1880.[84]

The ardent eighties, as an American writer calls the busy decade between 1880 and 1889, was a time when internal and external factors began the end of the American traditional isolationism in international affairs, increasing immigration, industrial expansion, the disappearing of the frontier, and a growing interest and activity in matters outside the national borders. The expansion movement was

---

[82] Henry Otis Dwight et al., The Encyclopedia of Missions *Descriptive, Historical, Biographical, Statistical*, New York, Funk & Wagnals Co. 1904.

[83] Winfred Ernest Garrison, *The March of Faith*, New York, Harper & Brothers, Publishers, 1933, p, 184.

[84] Dwight et al., *op. cit..*, p. 607.

reflected not only in economic and military aspects, but also in missionary adventures.[85]

It was especially true in the Caribbean area that a "generous scattering of seed" was witnessed during the years from 1880 to 1890.[86] Boards of foreign missions also initiated activity in Central and South America, penetrated the rest of the Spanish empire in America, and began to work with a new enthusiasm in the Dominican Republic, for a long time left as a field without missionary endeavor. In those years a notable increase of membership was observable in the Protestant denominations of the United States, and a series of young people's activities stirred the nation with their evangelistic campaigns.[87]

Puerto Rico was untouched by American Protestants, as has already been indicated, up to 1898, when its doors were open for foreign preachers after the Spanish defeat in San Juan. On Santo Domingo, in spite of the freedom of religion existing since 1844, American foreign boards did not attempt to perform any intensive work until about the same time as in Puerto Rico. Apart from the limited penetration of the African Methodists in 1846, largely among Dominican

---

[85] Robert H. Nichols, *The Growth of the Christian Church*, Philadelphia, The Westminster Press, 1941, p. 365.

[86] Wesley Amundswen, *The Advent Message in Inter-America*, Takoma Park, Washington, D.C.., Review and Herald Publishing Association, 1947, p. 78.

[87] Nichols, *op. cit.*, p. 366.

Negroes,[88] and the work of the Free Methodists in 1889 through the personal interest of a self-supported missionary,[89] nothing was done in this field prior to the late nineties, and that mostly after the imperialistic fever of 1898.

Cuba, due to a series of peculiar circumstances, became a focus of American religious forces during the last two decades of the nineteenth century. In this island the most representative denomination of the American Protestant Church have worked since 1883, though sporadic attempts were made as early as 1871, as indicated earlier in this paper.

The penetration of American Protestantism in Cuba, particularly after 1895, has been remarked as linked with imperialistic motives by one student of the movement.[90] For this author, a similar impulse moved the American churches in 1865 and in 1898, when those same American Protestant congregations wanted to "assist in the transfiguration of a conflict into a crusade for righteousness and humanity".[91]

The extinction of the old frontier, and the growing of American cities were, for Merle Curti, some of the reasons

---

[88] Beach and Saint John, *op. cit.*, p. 20. I have been unable to obtain similar information about the American board of foreign missions. The headquarters of this orgnization in Atlanta, Georgia, failed to supply information.

[89] Kenneth S. Latourette, *The Great Century*, New York, Harper & Brothers, 1943, V. 5.

[90] Garrison, *op. cit.*, p. 166.

[91] *Ibid.*

certain religious leaders had to fight for a militant missionary movement abroad.[92] Men like Josiah Strong, Congregationalist preacher, in his book "Our Country", advocated a religious expansion over seas in 1886.[93] To this can be added the specifically military incentive given by Captain Alfred T. Mahan to the imperialistic movement of the nineties. In regard to Cuba, the words of Mahan are a clear invitation to the occupation of the island by American naval forces,[94] pressumably to be followed by civilians with all the implements of American culture, homes, schools, and churches. The idea of giving Cuba a moral re-education after the conclusion of the Hispanic-American war, was frankly expressed by writers like Andrew S. Draper. "Until Cuba can set up a government of her own", he says, "we are bound to send to her schools and missionaries, and the other instrumentalities of moral and intellectual progress."[95] According to this writer, the American specific obligations would not be accomplished in that Antille until Cubans were able to secure, among other freedoms, religious freedom.[96]

---

[92] Merle Curti, *The Growth of American Thought*, New York, Harper & Brothers, 1943, p. 669.

[93] Charles A. Beard and Mary R. Beard, *A Basic History of the United States,* Philadelphia, The   Blakiston Company, 1944, p. 339.

[94] Cap. Alfred T..Mahan, *The Interest of America in Sea Power, Present and Future.* Boston, Little, Brown and Co., 1898, p. 310.

[95] Andrew S. Draper, *The Rescue of Cuba*, Boston, Silver, Burdett and Company, 1899, p. 180.

[96] Ibid,., p. 1'79.

V

AMERICAN PROTESTANTISM IN SANTO DOMINGO

Santo Domingo was the first country in the Spanish Antilles to enjoy religious toleration, and one of the first to enjoy such a freedom in Latin America. The circumstances of their early freedom from Spain secured that right in the first quarter of the nineteenth century. The men who came to lead the country during that early period of independence were people of liberal ideas educated under the influence of the French and American revolutions. The Haitian occupation of a few monhs after that independence, in 1822, if political arbitrary, indirectly favored the Protestant movement in a country for so many years closed to that kind of religious activity. Then began an era of twenty-two years under the regime of Boyer, the Haitian leader who subjugated the entire island.

In order perhaps to develop wider support in his newly aquired areas, Boyer decided to enlarge the Negro population of the Spanish side of the island by bringing free Negroes from the United States with the purpose of setting them in some areas of that territory, and sent a special representative to North America in 1824 with full instructions to obtain some thousands of colored colonists, freedmen ready to come to the Dominican part of the island with their families. The agent was Jonathan Granville, a well mannered and educated mulatto who arrived in New York in May of that year. Granville delivered some speeches before philantropic societies and held interviews with American authorities, and finally secured a goodly number of immigrants.[97]

The proposal of President Boyer, as they were explained by his agent Mr. Granville, sounded attractive to many Americans. Travel expenditures were to be paid by the Haitian government and thirty-six acres of land were offered to each of the immigrants. In addition, they were given full civil rights in the new country and economic support for four months.[98]

According to Granville, the American immigrants, almost all of them affiliated with the Protestant church, were to

---

[97] John Edward Baur, "Jean Pierre boyer and the Haiti of his day", *The Journal of Negro History*,. 32:307-353, October 1947.

[98] Mary Treudley, *The United States and Santo Domingo, 1789-1866*, Worcester, Mass., 1916, p. 224.

enjoy absolute tolerance in their religious beliefs and domestic habits, "provided they do not seek to make proselytes, or trouble those who profess another faith than their own".[99]

Boyer's plan for American colonists was welcomed by a writer in the *North American Review* who considered that "nothing can be more fair and honorable, or indicate a better spirit, than the part which President Boyer has acted, respecting the emigration of our people of color to that country."[100]

In August 23 of 1824 the first thirty Negro families sailed from Philadelphia under Granville's direction. Other groups of colonists from New England followed shortly. Several of them were destined for the city of Santo Domingo, where the first immigrants arrived in November. Others went to Samaná, and still others to Puerto Plata, all in Dominican territory. Nevertheless, as early as 1825 two hundred of them returned to the United States, disgusted with the habits of Haitians, or not adapted to rural life, since many of the colonists came from American cities without any previous training in agricultural work. A number of them became disappointed, vainly expecting continued support from the government of Haiti, others contracted

---

[99] Free Methodist Church of North America, General Missionary Board. Letter to the author of this thesis, Winona Lake, Indiana, August 2,,1950.

[100] "Correspondence relative to the Emigration of Free People of Color in the United States". *North Americm Review*, 20: p. 206, March 1825.

epidemic fevers, and the rest of them were not able to overcome lingual, religious, and social differences.[101]

In 1827 Benjamin Laundy visited Santo Domingo. This abolitionist and missionary has left an account of his observations. At that time, according to Lundy, there were almost eight thousands American people in the several sections of the island. He observed that quite a number of them had prospered, and enjoyed some influence among the native people. Besides, Lundy affirmed, some native converts had already been added to the original immigrants through the missionary efforts of the American Negroes.[102]

There is not much available material on the individual American colonies in Santo Domingan lands, but it is possible to describe the general development of them.

Those arriving in Santo Domingo city were provided with the old Catholic temple of San Francisco in which to perform their Protestant Services. This building was an abandoned cathedral which did not long endure its new role. In 1869 an American traveler reported the cathedral was a total ruin where plants and animals had taken the place of altars and furniture.[103] According to Rodriguez Demorizi, the group at Samaná "constituted" the church in 1824,

---

[101] John Edward Baur, *op. cit.*, p. 327.

[102] *Ibid.*, p. 235.

[103] De Benneville Randolph Kelm, *SKETCHES OF San Domingo*, Philadelphia, Claxton, Remsen & Haffelfinger, 1870, p. 235.

though a new temple was under construction in 1869.[104] The chapel of the American congregation at Puerto Plata was erected in June, 1835.[105]

In 1832 when the English Methodist missionary Theophile Pugh happened to come from the Turkish Islands to visit Dominican territory, some twenty-four American colonists of Puerto Plata sent him a letter asking him for a permanent English-speaking preacher from whom to receive the message of the Bible.[106] Pugh himself was not able to remain there as a permanent preacher, but he was a loyal mediator between them and the mother church at Turkish Islands. He also received other applications of the same kind from the American Protestants at Samaná and Santo Domingo City, and two years later, in 1834, the English missionary John Tindall was appointed for the ministry of Puerto Plata, though he was also a traveling pastor for Samaná and Santo Domingo City.[107]

Tindall was a young pastor who worked indefatigably until 1839, the year he ended his missionary labors. It was he who organized the Methodist Society of Samaná in 1835

---

[104] Luis M. Sears, "Frederick Douglas and the Mission to Haiti". *Hispanic American Historical Review*, XXI: 229.

[105] Dr. Cates Pressoir, *Le Protestantism Haitien*, Societe Biblique et des Livres Religieux, Port-au-Prince, Haiti, 1945, p. 157.

[106] *Ibid.*, p. 156.

[107] *Ibid.*, p. 159.

with a total of sixty members. Some months before he had founded his home-church at Puerto Plata.[108]

The whole colony of American Negroes was composed of Methodists and Baptists. According to Carol Morgan the Anerican Churches refused to send American preachers to those Negroes colonists in 1824[109], though Pressoir relates that some missionaries from Atlanta were sent to those English-speaking immigrants a little later.[110]

In 1838, after three years under the spiritual guidance of the Englishman John Tindall, the American colony at Puerto Plata received the visit of Reverend William Tower, also an English Wesleyan who worked in that mission until 1853, the year he died and was buried at the same town, after a labor which made him "beloved by all who knew him".[111]

According to J. Dennis Harris, who visited that mission in 1860, the American congregation was still alive, and was "by foreigners, comparatively well attended". Far from the optimism of Lundy, the American preacher touring the mission in 1827, Harris asserted that his countrymen had not

---

[108] *Ibid.*, p. 157.

[109] Carol McAfee Morgan, *Rim of the Caribbean*, New York, Friendship Press, 1942, p. 48.

[110] Pressoir, *op. cit.*, p. 49.

[111] J. Dennis Harris, *A summer on the borders of the Caribbean sea*, New York, A. B. Burdick, Publisher, 1860, p. 67.

converted a single native since the beginning of the colony.[112]

The Protestants of Puerto Plata had organized a manual-labor school, though it was not open after 1858. In 1860, the year of Harris' voyage, a new English missionary was coming to take charge of the Puerto Plata station.[113]

There is more information on the Samaná mission since this place was more often visited by Americans during the last century, and its geographical situation was widely studied by different nations interested in its possession. The town of Samaná was situated on the coast of a fine bay, the commercial and military advantages of which provoked the ambition of the United States, France, and England during the past century. In 1861 the population of the entire penninsula of Samaná was 1,721 inhabitants, and some three hundred of them belonged to the original American families.[114]

A Spanish lieutenant, Luis J. Golfi, in a survey made in May, 1861, described the religious aspect of that society saying that the most popular religion was the Catholic, although the Protestant sect had a good temple served by a mulatto minister supported by the English government. The Spanish official added that the Protestant church, in spite of the small number of its members, was the most sincerely

---

[112] *Ibid.*, p. 63

[113] *Ibid,.* p. 64.

[114] Demorizi, *op. cit.*, p. 149.

professed in town, and wisely served by a diligent preacher who made notable efforts to extend the Faith, delivering free copies of Bibles "without marginal notes" to the people, and having some influence in the country.[115]

The group of Samaná, like the other two missions, enjoyed a fairly tolerant attitude on the part of the Dominican or Haitian authorities. But it was different during the period of the Spanish re-occupation of Santo Domingo. Then came a time of trouble with the Spanish government, which transformed the Wesleyan church of Samaná into a military hospital. After some arguments on the legality of its status, the Spanish authorities declared the church illegal, since no freedom of worship did ever exist in the Spanish dominions. This attitude of the Spaniards cost the American negroes many misfortunes, and made them sincere advocates of Dominican independence in 1865.[116]

Frederick Douglass, the famous American Negro preacher and abolitionist, visited the mission of Samaná in 1869, and presented a collection obtained on board his ship to erect a new temple for that congregation.[117]

In 1875, as reported by the newspaper "La Opinión" of Santo Domingo, the condition of the American colony in Samaná was good, and their temple "pretty and well

---

[115] *Ibid.*, p. 162.
[116] *Ibid.*, p. 34.
[117] Sears, *op. cit.*

conserved", looking much better than the Catholic house of worship.[118]

The first missionary work organized by American Protestant among white people in Santo Domingo, and the last important movement initiated by North American denominations in that territory, took place in 1889, through the personal interest of a businessman from Ashtabula, Ohio. This man was Mr. Samuel E. Mills, a convert of the Free Methodist Church "who felt a call to missionary service and, learning of a great need of the Gospel on the island of Haiti, disposed of his business and with his wife and two small children took passage for the island".[119]

Mr. Mills was an honorary member of the Free Methodist Board, committee created in 1860 after a group of the Methodist Episcopal Church separated from the mother church "looking toward a more original Methodism".[120]

After a trip to Haiti, Mr. Mills observed that some Protestant Churches were already operating in the black republic, meanwhile the people in Santo Domingo were destitute of evangelical propaganda, except the original colonies of American Negroes. From 1889 to 1893 M. Mills developed a self-supported campaign in the towns of Monte-

---

[118] Demorizi, *op.cit.*, p. 40.

[119] Free Methodist Church of North America, General Missionary Board. A letter to the author of this thesis from Miss Mabel W. Cook, Research Secretary of the central offices of Winona Lake, Indiana, August 2, 1950.

[120] *Year Book of the American Churches*, 1937 Edition, Edited by Herman C. Weber, Associated Press, New York, 1937.

Cristi, on the north-west coast of the island. And a little later to the city of Santiago. Without a cent from the Missionary Board of his church, Mr. Mills and his wife traveled through the Cibao Valley, "singing and preaching, teaching English classes until more than 200 converts were gained".[121]

In 1893 Miss Esther D. Clark, also from Ohio, was sent as a formal Missionary under the care of the Free Methodist Church, though with "a small salary". She opened a school for Dominican girls in the town of San Francisco de Macoris. This work continued without much support until 1907, when the Central Headquarters at Winona Lake re-organized the work on a wider economic basis.[122]

---

[121] Free Methodist Church, letter to author of this thesis.

[122] *Ibid.*

VI

AMERICAN PROTESTANTISM IN CUBA

The history of Cuba cannot be properly written without wide reference to Key West. That small territory was particularly bound to the Greater Antille after 1868, the first year of the revolution initiated in Cuba by Carlos Manuel de Céspedes. At that time hundreds of Cubans moved to the Key, and some of them brought their own businesses with them. That migration was to have great significance in the political fate of Cuba. And from the religious viewpoint its role was also remarkable, because in that American key, the Cubans were to receive, for the first time, the Protestant doctrines, and to serve as ambassadors of the new faith in their own country.

The Episcopal Church was the pioneer among the American Protestant denominations interested in missionary work among Cuban exiles in Key West after 1868, although it was not until 1875 that Rev. John Freeman Young, elected bishop of the Episcopal Church in Florida, came down to Key West to pay a visit to his congregation.[123] At that time, due largely to the political influence of the Cuban immigration, a distinguised leader of those exiles was nominated Mayor of Key West. He was Carlos Manuel de Céspedes Jr., the only son of the Cuban revolutionary chief then fighting for the independence of his native land.[124] He and some other prominent Cubans in Key West met Bishop Young in December, 1875, and "informed him of the very general desire on the part of their people, now numbering over five thousand, the establishment of the Episcopal Church there in Spanish language".[125]

Céspedes himself, and some other distinguished Cubans were then received in the Episcopal Church, under the guidance of Juan B. Báez, a converted Cuban who became ordained Pastor for that Spanish-speaking congregation in January, 1879, after serving as a lay reader since 1875. This congregation, which began with 200 members in 1875, "gradually fell off", and was practically ended in the nineties after the death of Rev. Baez.[126] The church was called "Saint John", though it used the "Saint Paul" temple after the

---

[123] Edgar Legare Pennington, "The Episcopal Church in Florida, 1763-1892". *Historical Magazine of the Protestant Episcopal Church*, VII: 56, March 1938.

[124] *Ibid.*

[125] *Ibid.*

[126] Jefferson B. Browne, *Key West, the Old and the New*, St. Augustine, The Record Company, 1912, p. 31.

conclusion of the regular morning service of the English-speaking group.

The Rev. John L. Steele was also another notable leader in the Episcopal work among the Cubans of Key West until his death in 1878. The congregation reached its top number in 1879. There were then three hundred souls, representing seventy-two families worshipping there.[127]

Methodism had been active among Cubans of the Key since 1870, when the Florida conference of the then Methodist Episcopal Church South appointed Rev. Charles A. Fulwood to the pastorate of that territory. He saw the Cubans like "sheep without a shepherd", and began a missionary activity of lasting consequences among them.[128] In 1877 the Cuban Methodist Mission, organized some time before, was inaugurated. It was through the personal efforts of Rev. J. C. Ley, of the First Methodist Church of Key West that a credit of one thousand dollars was voted by the Methodist Missionary Society, and a lot was purchased on the corner of Duval and Angela streets. There the new temple was erected, and Henry B. Someillan was designated as its pastor, with Aurelio Silvera as his assistant.[129]

Among the Methodist workers in the Cuban colony of Key West was an active woman, Miss Annis Pyform, a well

---

[127] Pennington, *op.cit.*, p. 57.

[128] Elmer I. Clark and Harry C. Spencer, *Latin America U.S.A.*, New York, Board of Missions and Church extension, The Methodist Church, 1942, p. 53.

[129] Browne, *op. cit.*, p. 42.

educated lady who had devoted many years to help Cubans through a Methodist parish school in that Key.[130]

The first appearance of Baptist activity in that southern community took place in the autumn of 1879, the year that Rev. William F. Wood arrived in Key West to start the labors of his denomination there.[131] This American preacher converted a Spanish speaking woman, Miss Adela Fales, whose interest in the work among Cuban exiles gave basis to the creation of a Baptist mission for the Latin colony. That mission, supervised by Rev. Wood and successfully assisted by Miss Fales, furnished the connecting-link between the Home Mission Board of the Southern Baptist Convention and the Cuban mission inaugurated in Havana some years later.[132]

The activity of Rev. Wood, as it is developed in further pages of this paper, was not confined to his evangelical work in American territory. He departed to Cuba in 1886 to organize a Baptist mission on the Southern Coast of the neighboring Antille.

With the exception of Díaz and Duarte[133], the two great native pioneers of the Protestant work in Cuba, whose initial activities were supported by people from New York and

---

[130] *Ibid*.

[131] *Ibid*., p. 44.

[132] Arthur T. Pierson, *The Miracles of Missions*, New Yrok, Funk & Wagnalls Co., 1895, p. 74.

[133] A full description of the work of these two Cubans is given later.

Philadelphia, it was the influence of Key West churches that was finally decisive in the propagation of Protestantism in the island.

The Florida congregations and their leaders were not always able to promote missionary activity in Cuba with the effectiveness and promptitude they wished. Reverend John F. Young, for instance, was greatly discouraged in 1883 when his efforts to supply the Cuban mission of Matanzas with money were in vain, after asking for help from the Foreign Committee of the Episcopal Board of Mission in that year. Nevertheless, a year later Rev. Young was able to obtain an appropiation of $3,000 yearly from that same church department.[134]

Methodists also sent their missionaries to Cuba with the direct support of Key West congregations. The appointment of Aurelio Silvera and Henry B. Someillan were approved by the Methodist Conference of Florida in 1883. Five years later 194 members of the Havana congregation signed an application addressed to the Methodist Church of Key West to secure the permanent establishment of Mr. Someillan in the Cuban mission.[135]

In 1888 the name of Cuba was placed on the list of the Foreign Mission held by the American Church Missionary

---

[134] Pennington, *op. cit.*, p. 70.

[135] *Convención Magna de Cristianos Evangélicos de Cuba*, edited by Concilio Cubano de Iglesias Evangélicas, Habana, Imprenta "Cuba Intelectual", 1942, p. 57.

Society under the care of the Protestant Episcopal Church.[136] However, by then the field officially attended had been explored and organized by personal actions of American Episcopal missionaries since 1871.[137]

To this church belongs the glory of being the first Protestant congregation to open missionary work in Cuba during the nineteenth century. There is no evidence that any other American denomination made earlier efforts to settle its missions in Cuba.

The initial impulse was due to Rev. Henry Benjamin Whipple, Bishop of the Protestant Episcopal Church of Minneapolis since 1859. A graduate from the School of Divinity of Cornell, Rev. Whipple became active in home and foreign missionary activities, mostly among the American Indians.[138] In 1871 he visited Cuba and his stay there was used by some English-speaking people in Havana interested in obtaining the necessary official permission from the Spanish authorities for the establishment of an Episcopal church in that city. Rev. Whipple failed in his intervention with the Spanish Governor in Cuba, and his good offices in behalf of the Anglo-American community did not crystalize at that time. However, he was able to hold

---

[136] Arthur R. Gray, *The New World*, New York, The Domestic and Foreign Missionary Society, 1920, p. 230.

[137] Robert McLean and Grace Patrie Williams, *Old Spain in New America*, New York, Association Press, 1916, p. 91.

[138] Who was who in America, edited by The A. N. Marquis Co., Chicago, 1943, V.1. p. 1331.

Protestant services on board an American vessel in Havana harbor, and in March 18, 1871, the first Episcopal service in Cuban territory was performed by him at the Prussian consulate in that city.[139]

On his return to the United States, Rev. Whipple convinced his church of the desirability of sending a missionary to Cuba to preach the Gospel to the foreign Protestant residents in Havana, and in October, 1874, the House of Bishops of the Episcopal Church dispatched the Rev. Edward Kenney to Havana with a plan to organize a branch of that denomination there.[140] The role of Reverend Kenney was arduous, and the perils suffered while preaching were many.[141] He largely acted as a chaplain for American, British, and German residents in Havana, whose consuls were permitted to hold Protestant services privately, under his guidance.[142] A report on his experiences in Cuba was published by Kenney himself, in 1878.[143]

In 1883 a Cuban layman, Pedro Duarte, started work as a colporteur in Matanzas, a colorful city in the North coast of the Island, some fifty miles from Havana. He was

---

[139] Convención Magna, etc., *op.cit.*, p. 55.

[140] Horace Kenney, "Letter to the Editor", *The Literary Digest*, XVII 730, July-December 1898.

[141] *Ibid.*

[142] Convención Magna, etc., *op.cit.*

[143] Edward Kenney, *Report of Our Mission in Cuba, October, 1874, to October, 1877*, Detroit, 1878, as quoted in Carlos M. Trelles, *Biblioteca Histórica Cubana*, 3 Vols., Matanzas, 1924, II: 337.

working in the service of a rich Episcopalian from Philadelphia, Mr. John Rhoads, an active and philantropic member of that church in the Quaker city.[144] But Duarte was not going to remain as a simple seller of Bibles and tracts. He soon organized a group of believers and the first meeting was held in August, 1883, following the ceremonies of the Episcopal Church. The mission was designated "Fieles a Jesús" (Faithful to Jesus), and it was the first Protestant church established outside the province of Havana.[145] The chapel was erected at 60 San Juan de Dios Street, Matanzas, and a small school was also created for poor children of the city.[146]

That was too much to be peacefully accepted by the Catholic authorities, and Duarte was to suffer imprisonment for his daring attitude amid a society traditionally dominated by one church. Once he was free, he decided to go to Philadelphia where he prepared himself for the pastorate by two years of work and study. In 1885 Duarte came again to Matanzas, but this time as a formally ordained pastor, and the Episcopal Church was definitely established.[147] Then he established an orphanage and in 1886 a religious periodical publication was launched under his leadership. It was "El

---

[144] Gray, *op.cit.*, p. 138.

[145] *Ibid.*

[146] Convencion Magna, etc., *op. cit.*

[147] Gray, *op.cit.*, p. 139.

Precursor", a magazine devoted "to the propaganda of the Protestant Episcopal Church of Matanzas".[148]

The personal work of Rev. Duarte, and his tenacity, made it possible to have a lively congregation, and to "attract many Cubans of honorable families". A contemporary Cuban historian considers Duarte a "noble patriot and a highly meritorious Cuban".[149]

In Havana Rev. Juan B. Baez had also been acting as an Episcopal preacher since 1884. During the absence of Duarte, Rev. Baez served as his substitute in Matanzas. Nevertheless, the Episcopal work in the capital of the island was not going to last as long as that in Matanzas, and the mission almost disappeared during the war of independence, from 1895 to 1898.[150]

The origin of Baptist missionary movement in Cuba has an interesting history of colorful and romantic heroism. The leading role of that courageous adventure was performed by a native graduate from the dental school of Havana, Alberto J. Diaz. As an insurgent against the colonial regime in Cuba, Diaz was in danger of capture by Spanish forces, and fled to the United States in 1880. Once in New York he came in contact with a Baptist Missionary who converted him, and within a short time he was baptized at the Willoughby

---

[148] Trelles, *op. cit.*, This magazine was published from 1886 to 1887.

[149] Benigno Souza, "Iconografía de la Guerra del 95", *Diario de la Marina*, Suplemento en Rotograbado, Habana, October 16, 1949, p. 4.

[150] Convencion Magna, etc., *op. cit.*

Church in Brooklyn, New York.[151] By 1882 he was again in his homeland, this time as a self-supporting preacher while working as a dentist in Havana. Some months later he found out that the Ladies' Bible Society of Philadelphia needed a colporteur for Cuba, and he obtained the job. That was for two years. In 1885 the Baptist Home Mission Board South, through the suggestion of the Baptists of Key West, took him under its care. Now Diaz was able to do valuable work for his religion, but not without opposition and hardship. As reported by Samuel Hazard after his trip to Cuba, there was not such vigilant opposition to Protestants in the island during the last two decades of the past century. Nevertheless, the yellow fever and the Catholic opposition were two dangerous enemies of his labor.[152]

In 1885 Pastor Diaz edited in Havana an illustrative booklet containing the principles, meaning, and history of the Baptist denomination he represented in Cuba.[153] From that year on his religious career was considered a miracle. In January, 1886, the first Baptist church was formally organized in Havana under his pastorate. One year later the congregation numbered 301, with four Sunday schools functioning in the city, and six men being prepared for

---

[151] Albert H. Newman, *A History of the Baptist Churches in the United States*, New York, The Christian Literature Co., 1894, p. 457.

[152] Arthur T. Pierson, *The Miracles of Missions*, New York, Funk & Wagnalls Co., 1895.

[153] Alberto J. Diaz, *Historia, Convenio y Reglamento de la Iglesia Reformada de la Isla de Cuba fundada por el misionero Alberto J. Diaz*, Habana, 1885, as quoted in Carlos M. Trelles, *op, cit.*

preaching.[154] The growth of that church was easily observed through the reports of Diaz to the mother church in the United States.

Among the public places in Cuba under the monopoly of the Catholic church were the cemeteries. To bury a person in Havana implied the fulfillment of Catholic requirements and observance of Catholic ceremonies. All this was wisely avoided for a Baptist cemetery in 1887.[155] In 1894 the Southern Baptist Convention of the United States paid seventy five thousand dollars for a fine building in the center of Havana, to be used as the central temple of the Baptist congregation there.[156] This building is still the main place of worship for the Baptists of Havana.

Diaz was, without a doubt, one of the most active and succesful missionaries in Latin America. His name was praised in several missionary magazines of this country, and one author called him "the apostle of Cuba" in the title of a book.[157]

At the same time that Diaz was acting in Havana, another Baptist Missionary was organizing a branch of that denomination in Cienfuegos, an important city on the south coast of Cuba. He was Rev. William F. Wood, who had

---

[154] Pierson, *op. cit.*, p. 75.

[155] Trelles, *op. cit.*, p. 338,

[156] Pierson. *op. cit.*, p. 70.

[157] Kerr B. Topper, *Diaz, Apostle of Cuba*.. Philadelphia, 1986, as quoted by Carlos M. Trelles, *op. Cit.*

started the Baptist work in Key West in 1879. According to a local history of Cienfuegos, Rev. Wood established his mission in December, 1886, and it is remarked that this was the first Protestant church ever established in the city, and that it was located in Castillo Street, between Gacel and Hourruitiner Streets.[158] In March, 1887, the first baptismal ceremony was celebrated there, and at the end of the year Rev. Wood made a formal application to the local authorities to buy some lots for a Baptist cemetery.[159]

Beside the chapel erected in Castillo Street, Rev. Wood esteblished a free school for white and colored children, and a native convert, don Juan Ponce, was appointed the principal of the new institution. In December, 1887, this Baptist school had twenty-nine white pupils and eighty-three colored.[160]

It was a native of Key West, Aurelio Silvera, who ventured to bring Methodism into Cuba during the Spanish regime there. He was born of Cuban stock, and was an ordained pastor among the Cubans of Key West for some years, preaching at the Methodist temple on the corner of Duval and Angela Streets.[161] Silvera started his work in Havana in 1884 when he visited that city as an unofficial

---

[158] Enrique Edo, *Memoria histórica de Cienfuegos*, Habana, Ucar Garcia y Cia., 1943, p. 640.

[159] *Ibid,*, p. 657.

[160] *Ibid.*, p. 42.

[161] Bowman, *op. cit.*, p. 42.

missionary. Like some other visitors to the island during the XIX century, he opened his first headquarter in his hotel room. There he was able to talk for several Sundays to small groups of young people about the meaning and plans of the Methodist church.[162]

In 1890 two American missionaries traveled to Havana, in order to observe the activities of Silvera, and to encourage and help his mission in Havana. They were Dr. J. J. Ransom, and Miss Rebecca Toland, former missionaries in Brasil and Mexico, respectively. They found that some definite results had been obtained from Silvera's efforts, and that his converts had already organized some Sunday schools and small daily schools for general instruction.[163]

An active Methodist preacher in Cuba was Rev. Clemente Moya, appointed missionary to the congregation of Havana in 1889. He created three Sunday schools in the capital of Cuba, and remained in the Island until the initiation of the war of independence, in 1895.[164] During the years of that conflict Rev. Moya labored in a Methodist church of New York, where he organized, on July 8, 1895, a series of meetings to collect money for the Cuban rebellion.[165]

---

[162] Clark and Spencer, *op.cit.*, pp. 54-55.

[163] *Ibid.*, p.55.

[164] Convención Magna, etc,., *op. cit.*, p. 57.

[165] Guillermo Cabrera."Hechos Olvidados", *Heraldo Cristiano*, Habana, XIII:15, December 1945. This article was published in a Presbyterian magazine of Havana, and was based

(continued...)

Presbyterians were not very active in Cuba before 1898. A Mr. Graybill came from Mexico to Havana in 1890 to talk to a group of native Protestants interested in organizing a permanent mission in that city.[166] From that initial meeting arrangements were made, and a convert of the Island, Evaristo P. Collazo, was finally ordained Pastor in Havana. In the following years Rev. Collazo established missions in Remedios and Santa Clara, in the central regiom of Cuba.[167] That was the work of the Southern branch of the Presbyterian Church. The Northern branch initiated its evangelistic campaign in Cuban territory after the American military occupation of the Island, and both denominations became united at the beginning of the twentieth century.[168]

The American Bible Society had an early, though brief, activity in Cuba in 1825. In that year, a Roman Catholic priest, Don Justo Valez, became the first distributor of Scriptures in the island. The Society wished to appoint him its permanent agent in Havana, which was declined by the priest. Notwithstanding, it is reported that new Bibles were shipped to Cuba during the following years through the

---

[165] (...continued)
on information obtained from the collection of "Patria", the revolutionary paper edited in New York by Cuban exiles in 1895-1898. The collection is in the National Library, Havana. A copy of "Heraldo Cristiano" is in possession of the author of this thesis.

[166] *The Encyclopedia of Missions*, p. 607.

[167] Convención Magna, etc., *op.cit.*, p. 63

[168] There are very few available publications containing information on the initial activities of the Presbyterian church in Cuba. This denomination seems to have been less aggressive than the other sects performing missionary work in this period.

hands of that dynamic seller. In 1827 Valez sent $300 to the Society in New York, as the product of his distribution that year.[169]

It is presumed that occasional shipments of Bibles and portions of the Scriptures reached Havana throughout that century. In 1880, answering the question asked by the American Tract Society about the facilities to spread Protestant literature in Cuba, the American consul in Havana informed them that those who venture to distribute such printed material in the Antilles were in danger of severe trial by the Spanish judges. The only possibilities were the distribution of propaganda among the personnel of foreign ships in the harbor of Havana.[170]

Some twenty years before, when two British Protestants dared to deliver evangelical tracts to some homes in Havana, they were put in jail, and escaped more severe punishment only because of the decisive intervention of the British consul.[171]

In 1882 a special agent of the American Bible Society was appointed to Havana, then in an atmosphere of quasi-

---

[169] *La Biblia en Español*, edited by Sociedad Bíblica Americana, Havana, Imprenta Heraldo Cristiano, 1943, p. 23.

[170] 49
Wesley Amundsen, *The Advent Message in Inter-America*, Takoma Park, Washington, D.C., Review and Herald Publishing Association, 1947, p. 24.

[171] George Truman, *Journal of Rachel Wilson Moore*, Philadelphia, Publisher, T. Ellwood Zell, 1867, p. 31.

tolerance.[172] Two years later Rev. A. James McKim was nominated as the representative of that Society in Cuba and it was during his term in the agency that a notable increase in the selling of Bibles took place.

Thus, there was little or no activity on the part of Protestant churches in the Spanish-speaking Antilles at the beginning of the nineteenth century. But by the end of that century the major Protestant organizations had established themselves there.

The impulse to this activity came largely from the United States. Some of it was due to the growing economic interest of North Americans in the islands and the migration of Protestants in the islands. Much of it was due to the missionary expansion in the second half of the century. Some of it originated with islanders who had taken temporary refuge in the United States to carry on the independence movement and incidentally to accept Protestantism and take it back to the native Antilles.

---

[172] *The Encyclopedia of Missions*, p. 24.

Otros libros publicados por Ediciones Universal en la
COLECCIÓN CUBA Y SUS JUECES

0359-6	CUBA EN 1830, Jorge J. Beato & Miguel F. Garrido
046-1	CUBA Y LA CASA DE AUSTRIA, Nicasio Silverio Saínz
048-8	CUBA, CONCIENCIA Y REVOLUCIÓN, Luis Aguilar León
049-6	TRES VIDAS PARALELAS, Nicasio Silverio Saínz
119-0	JALONES DE GLORIA MAMBISA, Juan J.E. Casasús
165-4	VIDAS CUBANAS - CUBAN LIVES.- (2 vols.), José Ignacio Lasaga
207-3	MEMORIAS DE UN DESMEMORIADO-Leña para fuego hist. Cuba, José García Pedrosa
243-X	LOS ESCLAVOS Y LA VIRGEN DEL COBRE, Leví Marrero
293-6	HISTORIA DE LA ODONTOLOGÍA EN CUBA(4 vols: (1492-1983), César A. Mena
3122-0	RELIGIÓN Y POLÍTICA EN CUBA DEL SIGLO XIX, Miguel Figueroa
347-9	EL PADRE VARELA. (Biografía forjador de la conciencia cubana), Antonio Hernández-Travieso
353-3	LA GUERRA DE MARTÍ (La lucha de los cubanos por la independencia), Pedro Roig
379-7	HISTORIA DE FAMILIAS CUBANAS (9 vols.), Francisco Xavier de Santa Cruz
411-4	LOS ABUELOS: HISTORIA ORAL CUBANA, José B. Fernández
425-4	A LA INGERENCIA EXTRAÑA LA VIRTUD DOMÉSTICA, Carlos Márquez Sterling
431-9	MIS RELACIONES CON MÁXIMO GÓMEZ, Orestes Ferrara
437-8	HISTORIA DE MI VIDA, Agustín Castellanos
483-1	JOSÉ ANTONIO SACO, Anita Arroyo
490-4	HISTORIOLOGÍA CUBANA /4 vols./ (1492-1980), José Duarte Oropesa
516-1	EL PERFIL PASTORAL DE FÉLIX VARELA, Felipe J. Estévez
518-8	CUBA Y SU DESTINO HISTÓRICO. Ernesto Ardura
532-3	MANUEL SANGUILY. HISTORIA DE UN CIUDADANO, Octavio R. Costa
558-7	JOSÉ ANTONIO SACO Y LA CUBA DE HOY, Ángel Aparicio
592-7	DOS FIGURAS CUBANAS Y UNA SOLA ACTITUD, Rosario Rexach
606-0	CRISIS DE LA ALTA CULTURA EN CUBA/INDAGACIÓN DEL CHOTEO, Jorge Mañach
624-9	HISTORIA DE LA MEDICINA EN CUBA(2 v.),César A. Mena y Armando Cobelo
647-8	REFLEXIONES SOBRE CUBA Y SU FUTURO, Luis Aguilar León
680-X	¿POR QUÉ FRACASÓ LA DEMOCRACIA EN CUBA?, Luis Fernández-Caubí

682-6	IMAGEN Y TRAYECTORIA DEL CUBANO EN LA HISTORIA 2 v. 1492-1958), Octavio R. Costa
690-7	CUBA Y SU CULTURA, Raúl M. Shelton
703-2	MÚSICA CUBANA: DEL AREYTO A LA NUEVA TROVA, Cristóbal Díaz Ayala
738-5	PLAYA GIRÓN: LA HISTORIA VERDADERA, Enrique Ros
743-1	MARTA ABREU, UNA MUJER COMPRENDIDA Pánfilo D. Camacho
747-4	LA HONDA DE DAVID, Mario Llerena
752-0	24 DE FEBRERO DE 1895: UN PROGRAMA VIGENTE, Jorge Castellanos
765-2	CLASE TRABAJADORA Y MOVIMIENTO SINDICAL EN CUBA / 2 vols.: 1819-1996), Efrén Córdova
786-5	POR LA LIBERTAD DE CUBA (una historia inconclusa), Néstor Carbonell Cortina
798-9	APUNTES SOBRE LA NACIONALIDAD CUBANA, Luis Fernández-Caubí
804-7	EL CARÁCTER CUBANO, Calixto Masó y Vázquez
832-2	TODO TIENE SU TIEMPO, Luis Aguilar León
860-8	VIAJEROS EN CUBA (1800-1850), Otto Olivera
875-6	HISTORIA DE CUBA, Calixto C. Masó (Leonel de la Cuesta, Ed.)
876-4	CUBANOS DE DOS SIGLOS: XIX y XX. ENSAYISTAS y CRÍTICOS, Elio Alba Buffill
886-1	ISLA SIN FIN (Contribución a la crítica del nacionalismo cubano), Rafael Rojas
945-0	CRONOLOGÍA HISTÓRICA DE CUBA (1492-2000), Manuel Fernández Santalices.
953-1	JOSÉ AGUSTÍN QUINTERO: UN ENIGMA HISTÓRICO EN EL EXILIO CUBANO DEL OCHOCIENTOS, Jorge Marbán
957-4	LOS GRANDES DEBATES DE LA CONSTITUYENTE CUBANA DE 1940, Edición de Néstor Carbonell Cortina
965-5	CUBANOS DE ACCIÓN Y PENSAMIENTO, Octavio R. Costa
980-9	HUELLAS DE MI CUBANÍA, José Ignacio Rasco
982-5	INVENCIÓN POÉTICA DE LA NACIÓN CUBANA, Jorge Castellanos
8-000-6	LA POLÍTICA DEL ADIÓS, Rafael Rojas
8-028-6	CONTRA VIENTO Y MAREA. PERIODISMO Y ALGO MÁS (Memorias de un periodista 1920-2000), José Ignacio Rivero
8-047-2	LA REVOLUCIÓN DE 1933 EN CUBA, Enrique Ros
8-051-0	MEMORIAS DE UN ESTADISTA. FRASES Y ESCRITOS EN CORRESPON DENCIA, Carlos Márquez-Sterling (Edición de Manuel Márquez-Sterling).

8-058-8 DE LAS FILOSOFÍAS DESTRUCTIVAS CONTEMPORÁNEAS: BERGSON, SARTRE Y OTROS ENSAYOS, José Sánchez-Boudy y Hortensia Ruiz del Vizo
8-067-5 CUBA: INTRAHISTORIA. UNA LUCHA SIN TREGUA,
Rafael Díaz-Balart
8-072-3 ENCUENTRO EN 1898. TRES PUEBLOS Y CUATRO HOMBRES (Cuba-España-Estados Unidos /Cervera-T. Roosevelt-Calixto García-Juan Gualberto Gómez). Jorge Castellanos
8-075-8 FÉLIX VARELA: PROFUNDIDAD MANIFIESTA I: Primeros años de la vida del padre Félix Varela Morales: infancia, adolescencia, juventud (1788-1821), P. Fidel Rodríguez
8-079-0 EL CLANDESTINAJE Y LA LUCHA ARMADA CONTRA CASTRO, Enrique Ros
8-095-2 MISCELÁNEA CUBANAS, Instituto Jacques Maritain de Cuba
8-117-7 MOMENTOS ESTELARES EN LA HISTORIA DE CUBA,
Emilio Martínez Paula
8-129-0 VIVIDO AYER (Leyendas y misterios de Cuba y La Habana),
Sergio San Pedro
8-131-2 LA VERDADERA REPÚBLICA DE CUBA, Andrés Cao Mendiguren
8-135-5 RETOS DEL PERIODISMO, Alberto Muller
8-154-1 CON EL RIFLE AL HOMBRO, Horacio Ferrer
8-157-6 50 AÑOS DE REVOLUCIÓN EN CUBA. EL LEGADO DE LOS CASTRO, Efrén Córdova (Ed.).
8-167-3 UNA MIRADA SOBRE TRES SIGLOS. MEMORIAS, Orestes Ferrara
8-196-7 CARLOS MANUEL DE CÉSPEDES: DE YARA A SAN LORENZO. LA LEALTAD Y LA PERFIDIA. EL BRIGADIER DE CAMBUTE, EL MÉDICO DE JIGUANÍ, Enrique Ros
8-199-1 PANORAMA DEL PROTESTANTISMO EN CUBA,
Marcos Antonio Ramos
8-211-4 CUBA: MAMBISES NACIDOS EN OTRAS TIERRAS, Enrique Ros
8-212-2 CUBA Y EL CAYO HUESO DE AYER, Alejandro Pascual
8-231-9 VICENTE GARCÍA, EL INCOMPRENDIDO MAYOR GENERAL CUBANO, Enrique Ros

www.ingramcontent.com/pod-product-compliance
Lightning Source LLC
Chambersburg PA
CBHW060341080526
44584CB00013B/873